OCEAN ANIMALS

SEA HORSES

by Mari Schuh

AMICUS | AMICUS INK

snout

skin

Look for these
words and pictures
as you read.

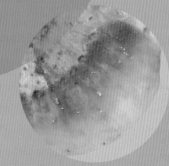

tail

pouch

A sea horse hides.
It looks like coral.
Can you find it?

Sea horses are fish.
They do not look like fish.
Their head looks like a horse head.

snout

Look at the snout.
It sucks up shrimp.
Slurp!

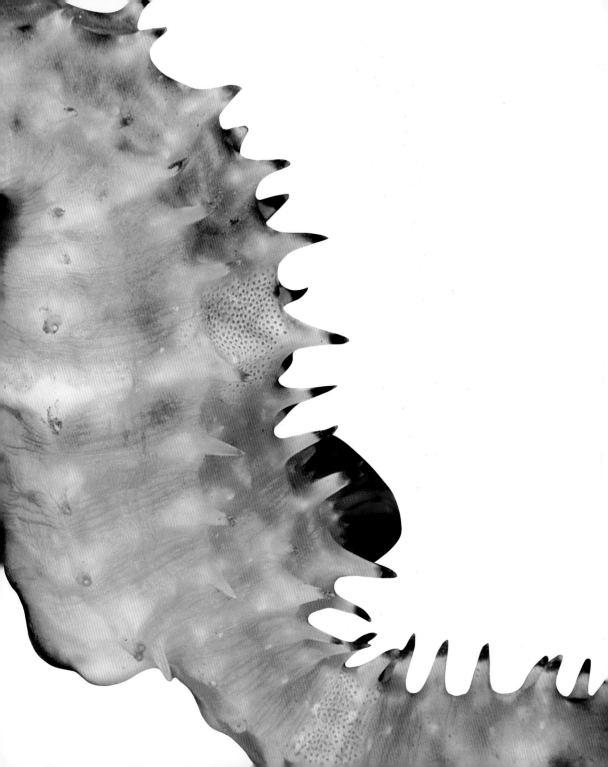

skin

Look at the skin.

Sea horses do not have scales.

Their skin covers bony rings.

Look at the tail.

It grabs seagrass.

The sea horse will not float away.

tail

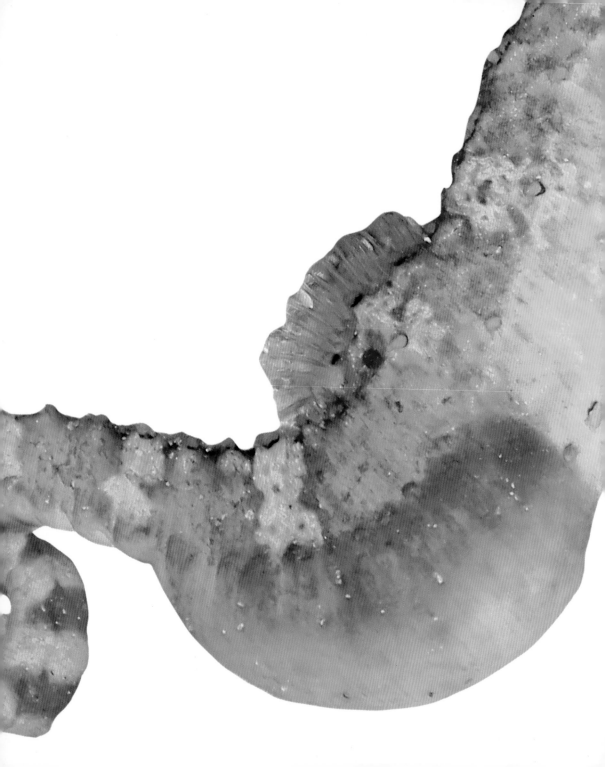

Look at the pouch.
Only males have a pouch.
Eggs grow in there.

pouch

Tiny babies are born.
They are the size of jelly beans.
They float away.

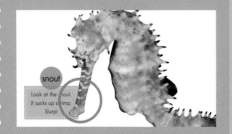

snout

skin

Did you find?

tail

pouch

Spot is published by Amicus and Amicus Ink
P.O. Box 1329, Mankato, MN 56002
www.amicuspublishing.us

Library of Congress Cataloging-in-Publication Data
Names: Schuh, Mari C., 1975- author.
Title: Sea horses / by Mari Schuh.
Description: Mankato, Minnesota : Amicus, [2020] | Series:
    Spot. Ocean animals | Audience: K to Grade 3.
Identifiers: LCCN 2018024628 (print) | LCCN 2018028132
    (ebook) | ISBN 9781681517131 (pdf) | ISBN
    9781681516318 (library binding) | ISBN 9781681524177
    (paperback)
Subjects: LCSH: Sea horses--Juvenile literature.
Classification: LCC QL638.S9 (ebook) | LCC QL638.S9 S36
    2020 (print) | DDC 597/.6798--dc23
LC record available at https://lccn.loc.gov/2018024628

Printed in China

HC 10 9 8 7 6 5 4 3 2 1
PB 10 9 8 7 6 5 4 3 2 1

Alissa Thielges, editor
Deb Miner, series designer
Ciara Beitlich, book designer
Holly Young, photo researcher

Photos by iStock/GlobalP cover, 16;
Shutterstock/BrunoGarridoMacias 1;
Shutterstock/Gerald Robert Fischer
3; Getty/Georgette Douwma 4–5;
Shutterstock/zaferkizilkaya 6–7; iStock/
GOLFX 8–9; Alamy/Andrey Nekrasov
10–11; Shutterstock/Rich Carey 12–13;
Minden/Shinji Kusano 14

SEA HORSES